Merry Christmas to

Dear Josh & Kenzie

and *From* Happy With

Engagement ♡ Love

Date

December 2016

Christmas Blessings

DONALD ZOLAN

HARVEST HOUSE PUBLISHERS

EUGENE, OREGON

Christmas Blessings

Artwork copyright © by The Zolan Company, LLC. All rights reserved.
Original oil paintings by Donald Zolan
Published by Harvest House Publishers
Eugene, Oregon 97402
www.harvesthousepublishers.com

ISBN 978-0-7369-5037-4

Donald Zolan: For information regarding art prints by Donald Zolan, please contact:
The Zolan Company, LLC, Donaldz798@aol.com; www.zolan.com

Design and production by Garborg Design Works, Savage, Minnesota

Harvest House Publishers has made every effort to trace the ownership of all poems and quotes. In the event of a question arising from the use of a poem or quote, we regret any error made and will be pleased to make the necessary correction in future editions of this book.

All Scripture quotations, unless otherwise indicated, are taken from The Holy Bible, *New International Version® NIV®*. Copyright © 1973, 1978, 1984, 2011 by Biblica, Inc.™ Used by permission. All rights reserved worldwide.

Verses marked NASB are taken from the New American Standard Bible®, © 1960, 1962, 1963, 1968, 1971, 1972, 1973, 1975, 1977, 1995 by The Lockman Foundation. Used by permission. (www.Lockman.org)

Printed in China
12 13 14 15 16 17 18 19 20 / FC / 10 9 8 7 6 5 4 3 2 1

Christmas Blessings

Angels from the Realms of Glory

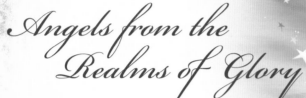

Angels from the realms of glory,
Wing your flight o'er all the earth;
Ye who sang creation's story
Now proclaim Messiah's birth.

Come and worship, come and worship,
Worship Christ, the newborn King.

JAMES MONTGOMERY

𝒯here were some shepherds staying out in the fields and keeping watch over their flock by night. And an angel of the Lord suddenly stood before them, and the glory of the Lord shone around them; and they were terribly frightened. But the angel said to them, "Do not be afraid; for behold, I bring you good news of great joy which will be for all the people; for today in the city of David there has been born for you a Savior, who is Christ the Lord. This will be a sign for you: you will find a baby wrapped in cloths and lying in a manger." And suddenly there appeared with the angel a multitude of the heavenly host praising God and saying,

"Glory to God in the highest, and on earth peace among men with whom He is pleased."

LUKE 2:8-14 NASB

WELCOME, ALL WONDERS IN ONE SIGHT!

ETERNITY SHUT IN A SPAN.

SUMMER TO WINTER, DAY IN NIGHT,

HEAVEN IN EARTH, AND GOD IN MAN.

RICHARD CRASHAW, "IN THE HOLY NATIVITY OF OUR LORD"

Whatever else be lost among the years,

Let us keep Christmas still a shining thing;

Whatever doubts assail us, or what fears,

Let us hold close one day, remembering

Its poignant meaning for the hearts of men.

Let us get back our childlike faith again.

GRACE NOLL CROWELL

Sweet souls around us watch us still,

Press nearer to our side;

Into our thoughts, into our prayers,

With gentle helpings glide.

HARRIET BEECHER STOWE

$\mathcal{W}$hen the angels had gone away from them into heaven, the shepherds began saying to one another, "Let us go straight to Bethlehem then, and see this thing that has happened which the Lord has made known to us." So they came in a hurry and found their way to Mary and Joseph, and the baby as He lay in the manger. When they had seen this, they made known the statement which had been told them about this Child. And all who heard it wondered at the things which were told them by the shepherds. But Mary treasured all these things, pondering them in her heart.

LUKE 2:15-19 NASB

O CHRISTMAS SUN! WHAT

HOLY TASK IS THINE!

TO FOLD A WORLD IN THE

EMBRACE OF GOD!

GUY WETMORE CARRYL

I will honor Christmas in my heart, and try to keep it all the year.

CHARLES DICKENS

Love came down at Christmas,

Love all lovely, Love Divine;

Love was born at Christmas,

Star and Angels gave the sign.

CHRISTINA ROSSETTI

Cut a path into the
heaven of glory,
Leaving a track of light
for men to wonder at.

WILLIAM BLAKE

O LOVELY VOICES OF THE SKY,

THAT HYMN'D THE SAVIOUR'S BIRTH!

ARE YE NOT SINGING STILL ON HIGH,

YE THAT SANG, "PEACE ON EARTH"!

FELICIA HEMANS

An angel can illuminate the thought and mind of man by strengthening the power of vision.

SAINT THOMAS AQUINAS

Angels descending, bring from above,
Echoes of mercy, whispers of love.

FANNY J. CROSBY

WE CARRY WITH US THE WONDERS

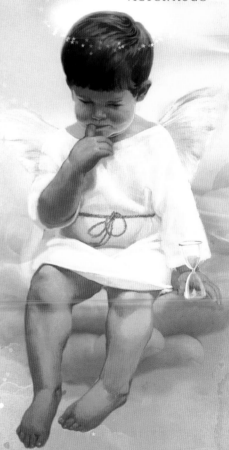

The beauty of the world and the orderly arrangement of everything celestial makes us confess that there is an excellent and eternal nature, which ought to be worshiped and admired by all mankind.

CICERO

HOPE IS THE WORD WHICH GOD HAS WRITTEN ON THE BROW OF EVERY MAN.

VICTOR HUGO

VE SEEK WITHOUT US.

SIR THOMAS BROWNE

I beheld a Virgin of extreme beauty well wrapped in a white mantle and a delicate tunic...with her beautiful golden hair falling loosely down her shoulders... She stood with uplifted hands, her eyes fixed on heaven, rapt, as it were, in an ecstasy of contemplation, in a rapture of divine sweetness. And while she stood in prayer, I beheld her Child move in her womb and... she brought forth her Son, from Whom such ineffable light and splendor radiated that the sun could not be compared to it... And then I heard the wonderful singing of many angels.

SAINT BRIDGET OF SWEDEN

O star of wonder, star of light,
Star with royal beauty bright,
Westward leading, still proceeding,
Guide us to thy perfect light.

JOHN H. HOPKINS JR., "WE THREE KINGS"

BOLDLY AND WISELY IN THAT LIGHT THOU HAST—
THERE IS A HAND ABOVE WILL HELP THEE ON.

PHILIP JAMES BAILEY

Ask and you will receive, and your joy will be complete.

JOHN 16:24

The rays of happiness, like those of light, are colorless when unbroken.

HENRY WADSWORTH LONGFELLOW

Love is patient, love is kind. It does not envy, it does not boast, it is not proud. It does not dishonor others, it is not self-seeking, it is not easily angered, it keeps no record of wrongs. Love does not delight in evil, but rejoices with the truth. It always protects, always trusts, always hopes, always perseveres. Love never fails.

1 CORINTHIANS 13:4-8

WHATEVER IS TO REACH THE HEART MUST COME FROM ABOVE.

LUDWIG VAN BEETHOVEN

For all we know

Of what the Blessed do above

Is, that they sing, and that they love.

EDMUND WALLER

It is good to be children

sometimes, and never

better than at Christmas

when its mighty Founder

was a child Himself.

CHARLES DICKENS

Teach us delight in

THE HEART THAT IS TO BE FILLED TO THE BRIM WITH HOLY JOY MUST BE HELD STILL.

GEORGE SEATON BOWES

There is nothing like a dream to create the future.

VICTOR HUGO

I believe that if one always looked at the sky, one would end up with wings.

GUSTAVE FLAUBERT

MUSIC IS WELL SAID TO BE THE SPEECH OF ANGELS.

THOMAS CARLYLE

simple things.

RUDYARD KIPLING

LET US NOT BE JUSTICES OF THE PEACE, BUT ANGELS OF PEACE. SAINT THERESE OF LISIEUX

Angels we have heard on high
Sweetly singing o'er the plains,
And the mountains in reply
Echoing their joyous strains.

Come to Bethlehem and see
Christ whose birth the angels sing;
Come, adore on bended knee,
Christ the Lord, the newborn King.

UNKNOWN AUTHOR, "ANGELS WE HAVE HEARD ON HIGH"

CHRISTMAS IS THE SEASON FOR KINDLING THE FIRE OF HOSPITALITY
IN THE HALL, THE GENIAL FLAME OF CHARITY IN THE HEART.

WASHINGTON IRVING

*I*f I have freedom in my love,

And in my soul am free,

Angels alone that soar above,

Enjoy such liberty.

RICHARD LOVELACE

IF INSTEAD OF A GEM, OR EVEN A

FLOWER, WE SHOULD CAST THE GIFT

OF A LOVING THOUGHT INTO THE

HEART OF A FRIEND, THAT WOULD BE

GIVING AS THE ANGELS GIVE.

GEORGE MACDONALD

I cannot be content

with less than heaven.

PHILIP JAMES BAILEY

Light tomorrow with today.

ELIZABETH BARRETT BROWNING

EVERY MOMENT IS A GOLDEN ONE

FOR HIM WHO HAS THE VISION

TO RECOGNIZE IT AS SUCH.

HENRY MILLER

JOYS ARE
OUR WINGS.

JEAN PAUL RICHTER

*G*ratitude is a nice touch of beauty added last of all to the countenance, giving a classic beauty, an angelic loveliness, to the character.

THEODORE PARKER

*H*ope is that thing
with feathers that
perches in the soul and
sings the tune without
the words and never
stops...at all.

EMILY DICKINSON

AN ASPIRATION IS A JOY FOREVER.

ROBERT LOUIS STEVENSON

IN THE MORNING, LORD, YOU HEAR MY VOICE;

IN THE MORNING I LAY MY REQUESTS BEFORE

YOU AND WAIT EXPECTANTLY.

PSALM 5:3

Hope is like the wing of
an angel, soaring up to heaven,
and bearing our prayers to the
throne of God.

JEREMY TAYLOR

*The sight of
the stars makes
me dream.*

VINCENT VAN GOGH

You make known to me the path of life;

you will fill me with joy in your presence.

PSALM 16:11

It is heaven upon earth to have

a man's mind move in charity,

rest in providence, and turn

upon the poles of truth.

FRANCIS BACON

FOR CHRIST IS BORN OF MARY,

AND GATHERED ALL ABOVE,

WHILE MORTALS SLEEP,

THE ANGELS KEEP THEIR

WATCH OF WONDERING LOVE.

PHILLIPS BROOKS

I will honour Christmas in my heart, and try to keep it all the year.

I will live in the Past, the Present, and the Future.

The Spirits of all Three shall strive within me.

I will not shut out the lessons that they teach.

EBENEZER SCROOGE, FROM CHARLES DICKENS' *A CHRISTMAS CAROL*

Every charitable act is a stepping stone toward heaven.

HENRY WARD BEECHER

THE EVENING STAR, LOVE'S HARBINGER, APPEARED.

JOHN MILTON

A single grateful thought towards heaven is the most perfect prayer.

EPHRAIM GOTTHOLD LESSING

LITTLE DEEDS OF KINDNESS,

LITTLE WORDS OF LOVE,

HELP TO MAKE EARTH HAPPY

LIKE THE HEAVEN ABOVE.

JULIA FLETCHER CARNEY

To see the world in a grain of sand, and to see heaven in a wild flower, hold infinity in the palm of your hands, and eternity in an hour.

WILLIAM BLAKE

The song of heaven is ever new; for daily thus and nightly, new discoveries are made of God's unbounded wisdom, love, and power, which give the understanding larger room, and swell the hymn with ever growing praise.

ROBERT POLLOK

Silently, one by one, in the infinite meadows of heaven,
Blossomed the lovely stars, the forget-me-nots of the angels.

HENRY WADSWORTH LONGFELLOW

HOME IS THE SPHERE OF HARMONY

AND PEACE. THE SPOT WHERE ANGELS

FIND A RESTING PLACE, WHEN BEARING

BLESSINGS THEY DESCEND TO EARTH.

SARAH J. HALE

BUT LET ALL WHO TAKE REFUGE IN YOU BE GLAD;
LET THEM EVER SING FOR JOY.
SPREAD YOUR PROTECTION OVER THEM,
THAT THOSE WHO LOVE YOUR NAME
MAY REJOICE IN YOU.

PSALM 5:11

Heaven is the day of which grace is the dawn, the
rich, ripe fruit of which grace is the lovely flower; the
inner shrine of that most glorious temple to which
grace forms the approach and outer court.

THOMAS GUTHRIE

Heaven, the treasury of everlasting joy.

WILLIAM SHAKESPEARE

HEAVEN LIES
ABOUT US IN
OUR INFANCY.

WILLIAM WORDSWORTH

*H*eaven's the perfection of all that can be said or thought— riches, delight, harmony, health, beauty; and all these not subject to the waste of time, but in their height eternal.

JAMES SHIRLEY

THE LOVE OF HEAVEN
MAKES ONE HEAVENLY.

WILLIAM SHAKESPEARE

Heaven will be the endless portion of
every man who has heaven in his soul.

HENRY WARD BEECHER

I try to avoid
looking forward
or backward,
and try to keep
looking upward.

CHARLOTTE BRONTË

O welcome, pure-eyed Faith, white-handed Hope,

Thou hovering angel, girt with golden wings!

JOHN MILTON

I have always thought of Christmas time, when it has come round, as a good time; a kind, forgiving, charitable time; the only time I know of, in the long calendar of the year, when men and women seem by one consent to open their shut-up hearts freely, and to think of people below them as if they really were fellow passengers to the grave, and not another race of creatures bound on other journeys.

CHARLES DICKENS

OUR HEARTS GROW TENDER WITH CHILDHOOD MEMORIES AND LOVE OF KINDRED, AND WE ARE BETTER THROUGHOUT THE YEAR FOR HAVING, IN SPIRIT, BECOME A CHILD AGAIN AT CHRISTMAS-TIME.

LAURA INGALLS WILDER

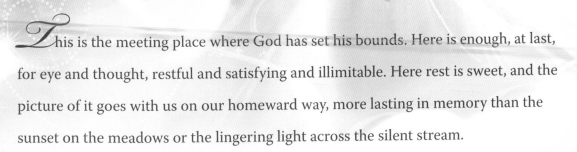

'Twas Christmas broach'd the mightiest ale;

'Twas Christmas told the merriest tale;

A Christmas gambol oft could cheer

The poor man's heart through half the year.

WALTER SCOTT

This is the meeting place where God has set his bounds. Here is enough, at last, for eye and thought, restful and satisfying and illimitable. Here rest is sweet, and the picture of it goes with us on our homeward way, more lasting in memory than the sunset on the meadows or the lingering light across the silent stream.

ISAAC OGDEN RANKIN

Silent night, holy night

Wondrous star, lend thy light;

With the angels let us sing,

Alleluia to our King;

Christ the Savior is born,

Christ the Savior is born!

JOSEF MOHR, "SILENT NIGHT"

GOOD NEWS FROM HEAVEN THE ANGELS BRING,

GLAD TIDINGS TO THE EARTH THEY SING;

TO US THIS DAY A CHILD IS GIVEN,

TO CROWN US WITH THE JOY OF HEAVEN.

MARTIN LUTHER

Of all dear days is Christmas Day
the dearest and the best.

MARGARET SANGSTER

IT IS CHRISTMAS IN
THE HEART THAT PUTS
CHRISTMAS IN THE AIR.

W.T. ELLIS

CHRISTMAS
IS THE DAY
THAT HOLDS
ALL TIME
TOGETHER.

ALEXANDER SMITH

It came upon the midnight clear,

That glorious song of old,

From angels bending near the earth,

To touch their harps of gold;

"Peace on the earth, good will to men,

From Heaven's all gracious King."

The world in solemn stillness lay,

To hear the angels sing.

EDMUND H. SEARS,
"IT CAME UPON THE MIDNIGHT CLEAR"

*I*t is the Christmas time:

And up and down 'twixt heaven and earth,

In glorious grief and solemn mirth,

The shining angels climb.

DINAH MARIA MULOCK

Blessed is the season which engages the whole world in a conspiracy of love!

HAMILTON WRIGHT MABIE

At Christmas a man is at his finest towards the finish of the year;

He is almost what he should be when the Christmas season's here;

Then he's thinking more of others than he's thought the months before,

And the laughter of his children is a joy worth toiling for.

He is less a selfish creature than at any other time;

When the Christmas spirit rules him he comes close to the sublime.

EDGAR GUEST

FAIL NOT TO CALL TO MIND, IN THE COURSE OF THE TWENTY-FIFTH OF THIS MONTH, THAT THE DIVINEST HEART THAT EVER WALKED THE EARTH WAS BORN ON THAT DAY; AND THEN SMILE AND ENJOY YOURSELVES FOR THE REST OF IT; FOR MIRTH IS ALSO OF HEAVEN'S MAKING.

JAMES HENRY LEIGH HUNT

GREAT
LITTLE ONE!
WHOSE ALL-
EMBRACING
BIRTH
LIFTS EARTH
TO HEAVEN,
STOOPS
HEAVEN TO
EARTH.

RICHARD CRASHAW

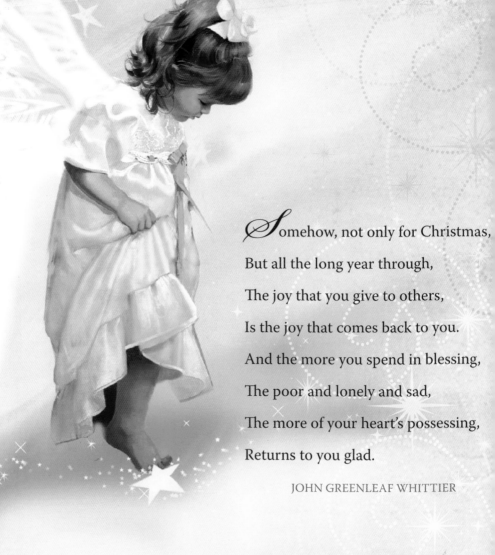

Somehow, not only for Christmas,

But all the long year through,

The joy that you give to others,

Is the joy that comes back to you.

And the more you spend in blessing,

The poor and lonely and sad,

The more of your heart's possessing,

Returns to you glad.

JOHN GREENLEAF WHITTIER

Hark! The herald angels sing,

"Glory to the newborn King!

Peace on earth, and mercy mild,

God and sinners reconciled!"

Joyful, all ye nations rise,

Join the triumph of the skies;

With th' angelic host proclaim,

"Christ is born in Bethlehem!"

CHARLES WESLEY,
"HARK! THE HERALD ANGELS SING"

*M*ay the spirit of Christmas bring you peace,

The gladness of Christmas give you hope,

The warmth of Christmas grant you love.

A CHRISTMAS BLESSING

Be merry all, be merry all,

With holly dress the festive hall;

Prepare the song, the feast, the ball,

To welcome merry Christmas.

WILLIAM ROBERT SPENCER

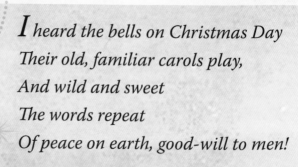

I heard the bells on Christmas Day
Their old, familiar carols play,
And wild and sweet
The words repeat
Of peace on earth, good-will to men!

HENRY WADSWORTH LONGFELLOW,
"I HEARD THE BELLS ON CHRISTMAS DAY"

O HOLY NIGHT, THE STARS ARE BRIGHTLY SHINING;
IT IS THE NIGHT OF THE DEAR SAVIOR'S BIRTH!

PLACIDE CAPPEAU, "O HOLY NIGHT"

*H*appy, happy Christmas, that can win us

back to the delusions of our childish days;

that can recall to the old man the

pleasures of his youth; that can

transport the sailor and the traveller,

thousands of miles away, back to his

own fire-side and his quiet home!

CHARLES DICKENS, *THE PICKWICK PAPERS*

AT CHRISTMAS-TIDE THE OPEN HAND

SCATTERS ITS BOUNTY O'ER SEA AND LAND,

AND NONE ARE LEFT TO GRIEVE ALONE,

FOR LOVE IS HEAVEN AND CLAIMS ITS OWN.

MARGARET ELIZABETH SANGSTER

O, beautiful rainbow, all woven of light! Heaven surely is open when thou dost appear, and bending above thee the angels draw near, and sign "The rainbow—the rainbow: the smile of God is here!"

MRS. S.C. HALL

When Christmas bells are swinging above the fields of snow, we hear sweet voices ringing from lands of long ago, and etched on vacant places are half-forgotten faces of friends we used to cherish, and loves we used to know.

ELLA WHEELER WILCOX

Sing, choirs of angels, sing in exultation;

O sing, all ye citizens of heaven above!

Glory to God, all glory in the highest;

JOHN F. WADE, "O COME, ALL YE FAITHFUL"

THE EARTH HAS GROWN OLD WITH ITS BURDEN OF CARE,

BUT AT CHRISTMAS IT ALWAYS IS YOUNG,

THE HEART OF THE JEWEL BURNS LUSTROUS AND FAIR,

AND ITS SOUL FULL OF MUSIC BREAKS THE AIR

WHEN THE SONG OF ANGELS IS SUNG.

PHILLIPS BROOKS

*E*very saint in heaven is
as a flower in the garden
of God, and holy love is
the fragrance and sweet
odor that they all send
forth, and with which
they fill the bowers of
that paradise above.

JONATHAN EDWARDS

The kings they came from out the south,
All dressed in ermine fine;
They bore Him gold and chrysoprase,
And gifts of precious wine.

The shepherds came from out the north,
Their coats were brown and old;
They brought Him little new-born lambs—
They had not any gold.

The wise men came from out the east,
And they were wrapped in white;
The star that led them all the way
Did glorify the night.

The angels came from heaven high,
And they were clad with wings;
And lo, they brought a joyful song
The host of heaven sings.

The kings they knocked upon the door;
The wise men entered in,
The shepherds followed after them
To hear the song begin.

The angels sang through all the night
Until the rising sun,
But little Jesus fell asleep
Before the song was done.

SARA TEASDALE

48